PLANE SONG

BY DIANE SIEBERT / PAINTINGS BY VINCENT NASTA

HarperCollins*Publishers*

through the skyways
touched by clouds
over highways
over crowds
roaring
soaring
at full tilt
go birds that human hands have built

planes that fly
from small dirt strips
from runways on the decks of ships
from giant airports
busy
bright
hustling
bustling
day and night

planes of every shape and size
that taxi out
take off
and
rise
above a world of
tundras
trees
fields and farmlands
cities
seas
humming
coming
through the day
toward horizons far away
moving through the star-filled night
winking
blinking
into sight
high above us in the sky
hear their engines!
see them fly!

jumbo jets whose engines roar
at 30,000 feet or more
ships of flight on waves of air
flying people everywhere

cargo planes with massive girth
moving goods around the earth

fire-fighting planes that go
over forests, flying low
above the trees and fire lines
dousing stands of burning pines

planes that fly through winds and rains—
hunters hunting hurricanes—
collecting data as they fly
through the whirlwind's peaceful eye

Navy planes with special gear
flying through the atmosphere
catapulted into flight
tail hooks down when they alight
on carriers designed to be
airfields floating out at sea

turbo props
commuter hops
folks in business suits
morning flight
return at night
on old familiar routes

chase planes
pace planes
escorting outer-space planes
high planes
sly planes
picture-taking spy planes

bush planes braving wind and hail
winging
bringing
goods and mail
to places others cannot go—
islands, jungles, lands of snow
planes equipped with big pontoons
to land on lakes or on lagoons
planes equipped with giant skis
to land and stand on snow with ease

planes for writing in the air
advertising with a flair

planes for dusting farmers' crops
skimming just above the tops
of fruits and vegetables and grains
that grow on fertile hills and plains

quick planes
slick planes
doing-fancy-trick planes
aerobatics in the sky
stalls and spins done way up high
hammerheads and barrel rolls
outside loops for hardy souls

planes called "rag bags"
rare old fliers
made of cloth and wood and wires

training planes for touch-and-goes
watch that airspeed!
drop the nose!

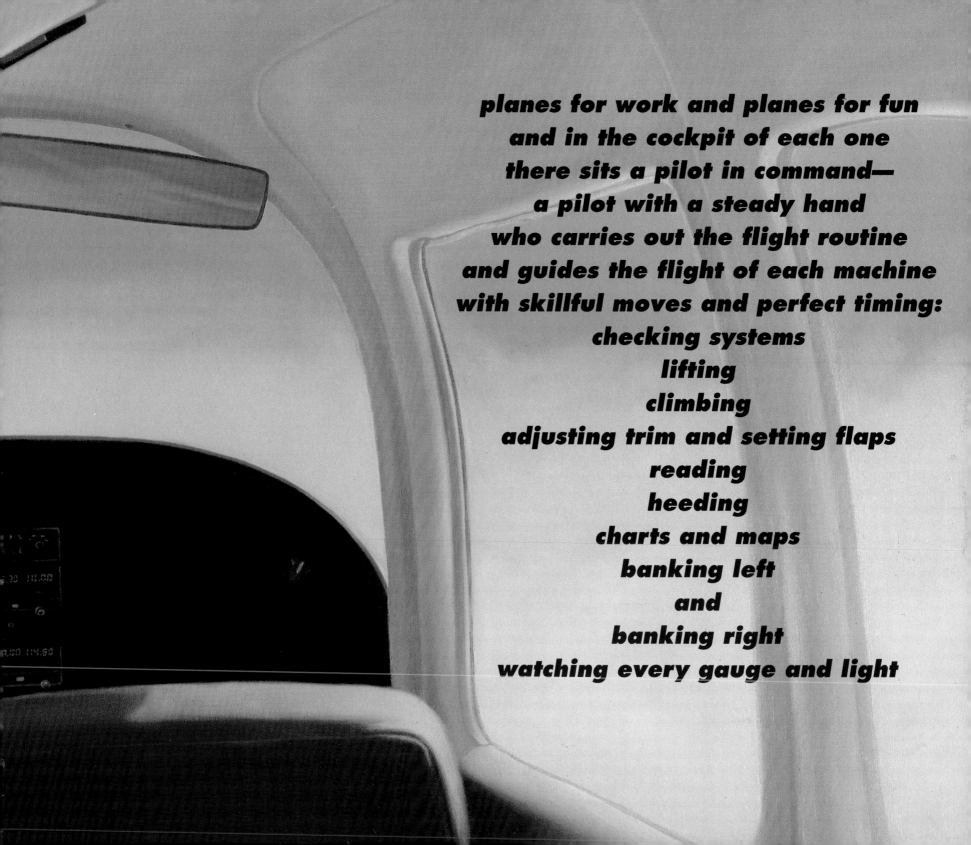

planes for work and planes for fun
and in the cockpit of each one
there sits a pilot in command—
a pilot with a steady hand
who carries out the flight routine
and guides the flight of each machine
with skillful moves and perfect timing:
checking systems
lifting
climbing
adjusting trim and setting flaps
reading
heeding
charts and maps
banking left
and
banking right
watching every gauge and light

while people on the earth below
watch airplanes come
and airplanes go
airplanes flying
way up there!
airplanes flying
way up where
the
soundless
boundless
skies invite
all those who spread their wings in flight

The illustrations in this book were painted with oils
on hardwood board.

Plane Song
Text copyright © 1993 by Diane Siebert
Illustrations copyright © 1993 by Vincent Nasta
Printed in Hong Kong. All rights reserved.
Typography by Al Cetta
❖

Library of Congress Cataloging-in-Publication Data
Siebert, Diane.
Plane song / by Diane Siebert ; paintings by Vincent Nasta.
p.   cm.
Summary: Rhymed text and illustrations describe different kinds of planes
and their unique abilities.
ISBN 0-06-021464-3. — ISBN 0-06-021467-8 (lib. bdg.)
ISBN 0-06-443367-6 (pbk.)
1. Airplanes—Juvenile literature.   [1. Airplanes.]   I. Nasta, Vincent, ill.
II. Title.
TL547.S524   1993   92-17359
629.133'34—dc20   CIP
                                                                 AC